ABC Moonlight

Ben Estes

The Song Cave

The Song Cave
www.the-song-cave.com

Design and layout by Janet Evans-Scanlon

ISBN: 978-1-7372775-3-8
Library of Congress Control Number: 2021948548

FIRST EDITION

All that you touch
And all that you see
All that you taste
All you feel
And all that you love
And all that you hate
All you distrust
All you save
And all that you give
And all that you deal
And all that you buy
Beg, borrow, or steal
And all you create
And all you destroy
And all that you do
And all that you say
And all that you eat
And everyone you meet
And all that you slight
And everyone you fight
And all that is now
And all that is gone
And all that is to come

And everything under the sun is in tune
But the sun is eclipsed by the moon

-Pink Floyd, "Eclipse"

Contents

Twelve Folded Poems

1.

Dear Nature,
did love make me?

2.

I'd had the idea to trace California
the same day the neighborhood burnt,
as some sort of daylight speech
(unlit until the night before)
had closed the eyes of every creature,
burnt through the graveyards,
and cooked all the snails
in all of the gutters.

1.

There wasn't yet a sun.
The sky was still empty.

The man who did this job
before me could stand so quietly.

He could make a whistle from the seed of any fruit.
Once he made a kite out of newspaper

and he told stories about the stars, and about the earth.
He told them to pass the night,

and because his heart was a reflection
in the soul of the world.

You would have loved him,
but it would have been more than that.

I started this without any answers.
I didn't have a choice.

I had not yet learned the terms for patience
or for holding hands.

I began at the beginning
when words were only pictures.

Later, I'd wait patiently with belief, and
type emails to distant friends.

I would walk in the woods,
sit down there, and turn

and hold the things I'd find.
Or, on some walks,

I'd take photos of flowers and mushrooms
with my phone. Who really cares.

Pull down the covers
pulse, erect, moon, leaf, smell,

listen through the walls.

2.

With empathy as the cornerstone
of good design, let's look there for meaning,
down into this sloping bowl of a field
funneling into my rainbow-painted tunnel.

Where was the nuance?

I got lost right here a few years back, and was risking
everything now by overreacting.
I reminded myself to never expose too much.
Similarly, the wordless relationship with
a snail I'd found as a child, under the porch.
Weak and introspective. It's silvery snail-trail
extraterrestrial. I'd tried then to match its slowness,
and my silly stillness made itself a human problem
without any human solution, shifting softly
into many other childhood illusions. Like now, how
lightning chips
bricks off my roof
one by one
in clumsy shatterings,
exposing the weakened structure
rebuilt too many times
by too many people
with too many conflicting ideas.
I tested each out as my own.
An architecture of decorative knots,
empty holes of hesitation

and pre-teen embarrassment
dressed up in my "gentle magician"
costume, wrong in assuming that
this was a special event.
I've now gone ahead and scheduled
a deep level sweep of my fireplace.
Throw in some clay, watch me turn it to glass.
If I had a bell, I'd ring it in the morning
I'd ring it in the evening, all over this land.

1.

It is a huge sound.

Rain on the leaves
of a forest
during a thunderstorm.

A noise
the color of the air.

Important glories grow
invisible at a distance
in the changing colors
of a transparent flower.

2.

Fold the circle.

Facing and touching,
learn liberty release.

1.

The sky separated from the earth.

A sky upon skies upon layers of skies,
a cloud upon clouds.
A man in a field,
a man on the side of a hill,
a man on a motorbike,
men in a kitchen,
a man on a gravel path,
all men in all weather,
each a human midnight
taking each day along with mine
to clasp a mutual sympathy,
to clasp with clumsy hate.

2.

The marsh rises over the earth.

I've not
created my own thoughts.
Distractions and shallow living
roll through the clamor of people.

1.

Will it die
once we've learned
enough of the world?
Recollections align
with experiences
far from the magazines
and museums, while the
selfish use sincerity
to impress the internet's
virtual friendscape.
Like native prairies
blackened and bleached.
Their promises an obligation.
For the complex giving of honor
to the artist, art is not just
anything.

2.

On foot and by ear – it'll sound
up from the ground with regularity.

Who rang the expectations
from summer thunders

above green apple canopies,
the rocks all ringing?

Ringing!
Around us.

All around!
And will reside in the air

& undergrowth, not to be
offered in some kind of trade, this

love is not merchandise, resting
within the strenuous

qualities of fire.

Now to let something go
of myself,

without any need
to replace it.

1.

Worse than the loss,
that life goes on.

He returns, you shine his little gold ring,
thinking something good might come of it,
but remain skeptical. The shame of the poor
states *patience is hope.* Facing my new illusion
in confusion and curses and blood,
this search for meaning
is too much for me today,
watching god, nature-less,
nature, unaware of the news.
The sound seemed to come from the sky.

Addressed to my feminine heart, was it a love song?
That you played on your translucent guitar?
To say you'll never forget is unfair.
Amid such sickness and chaos,
our hearts were only reflections.
Please, sing all of it as slow as this slowest part.

Our shared terms were:
tender and wild.
We were two fountains
connected by an underground river
running through the

frog-rich margins
emptying into the center of the earth.
We were two glass apples,
two hundred thousand pixels.
Two problems of an unseen rose
whose little expressions of relief unwhorled.
All of the things I loved were given.
We had everything,
and I no longer feared anything.

We were two clouds
with souls
we weren't afraid to bear.

Walking in silence, I reached the hills
and watched the hang gliders fly, as if
they were perfume sprayed into the air.
After a dozen trips,
those big sleepy flowers
lay where they fell.
Their dark tracings and
looping flights in the sky
above wildfires burning
through the towns, the hills,
the headlines
keeping careful count
of our same trees,
our same fields,
the flying winds
hot then chilly,

sleepy then watchful.
I wish my life I'd never seen it.
Mirrored on the opposite coast,
I recognized my fate,
though wondered if I
were too fragile to fulfill it.

Lest the blazes
should touch my hand,
endsport held me tight
in the physical mesh,
watching love
be the end of the roses.
It *steams* them.
Though there is still
the hope that something
can come from something...

My fingers traced
the manual work
of my unconscious, while
the illusions of the world
arranged themselves
around me through
a doubled surface to
repeat the sounding joy.

2.

Our long association
with humankind could be seen,
but how can we continue to
rely on that?
We laid down with
the softer music, that spoke
to both of our senses of injustice,
leaving us hollow and lonesome –
a distinctly un-wild tune
plucked out on a scarecrow's
nervous twelve-string.

Eventually, kindnesses replaced
our committed effort,
and through the loose
boards of the dam after storms
rushed occasional floods
that we'd use to wash
our clothes, our sheets, our held hands.

Footprints in the
garden bed under my window,
drones in the sky,
it takes a few months
to get used to these new ways.
Bellows roll deeply

from the hills, and I
make a regular pilgrimage
to this home-scatter,
the sounds disturbing
the water, and shifting
their goals as poorly
as I end up filling out
mine, fumbling in the breeze.
With tears in my eyes, I'm grateful
for my place, and it softens me.
Love, now a circle,
now a spinning wheel.

And I called its name
and it did not respond.
And then after a while,
I'd move on again, learning
each husband cartoon.
The blacksmith or the boxer,
the time traveler,
the painter, the mushroom
farmer – I delay
the times above, below, and within
to find these doubled hearts and arches.
Embarrassed, I couldn't fit
any more answers next to the hopes I'd
hid inside my shell.
Finally, the image I see
now of the woods might be reflected
in a nighttime text: "are you awake?"

•

I've picked a ball of love for thee
while out walking in the fog.
I'm just a stenciled silhouette.
I will dedicate everything I do to you
touching your cheek to my mouth,
the tiniest dribble of another still in my heart
ashamed not to finish.
Twisting life around to
thank the light for being light
and the dark for not being light at all,
for roses for not being heavy
and the rocks for being heavy.

And you, here
because you must want
something dumb to love
to love, near.

1.

Everything works out best for the eye too young,
the candle watching itself in the mirror studying its waxy form,
or the bubble, without a wall on which to hang.

2.

It is clear cold water
full of tiny snails.

It is sinking deeply
into the thin stuff of being,
until it's being
is being breathless.

It is the human/animal divide
that we no longer use for fortune.

It is all that remains
of our once flooded valley.

It is a field of straw.

I found a bone.

I found another bone.

That was all for today.

1.

I'll surely end up with an even
slower life than I had had
before this settling into –
alone, staring deeply into the glassy sky
holding some vulgar lucky charm
to throw on out
onto the rippling water –
in and out . . . in and out . . . up and down . . . in and out.
Sitting down . . . pulling it down . . . looking inside . . . bending down.

2.

The pond sounds of the rain continue,
though it's already stopped raining.
Drops sliding off
branches and down the thick trunks.
Baby-clean daisy-colored clouds.
How does one draw a rainbow?
It's the impending death
and rebirth of humankind that
bends the air's iridescent edge.

1.

Come on down from your hill in the dark.
Now that they see you, they'll know
the open meadows are safe.

Get here safely.

One light comes on above the lake.
One lamp on the prairie.

I strike my match and lift it slowly.
No wind.

Corn stalks sigh
as the moon looks away.
The world can be so difficult to do.

I will no longer ask for help
for anything.
Anything but these traced poems.

I wish they
were flowers.

2.

Rain clouds
of rose water

on the sky-side
of the smoke

are browning
around their edges.

Rust's now here
in the rainbow.

If I were you, moon,
I'd shrink down

to a grain of sand,
your clairvoyance

condensed, on the edge
of a dusty country road.

O moon,
lend me your thoughtful hand.

O my moon-moon,
we are now, all of us, lost.

1.

The rotting man's the first to sing

well-tuned,
well-sung,
well-spoken.

2.

The powdery flower sings of what it's seen:

the shortening of these nights,
the lengthening of these days,

la-lu, la-la, lu-lu

1.

There was only one
reddish star left.
An animal
captured it
in its mouth
and delivered it,
here.

"Humans will
lose their purpose,"
it says. Phew.

So this
is a Shepherd's Hour.
And, now, now,
our hearts held close
to the balance block,
we've come

& we've found

everyone.

2.

I will be wearing my yellow
winter hat, Tom,
because once we
have all gone
over

I will need you
to be able
to find
me.

1.

Won't it be lovely to walk home in the dark?
Like the silence when a movie ends

Like a machine of black metal and chains
Like pointillism

Like branches dropping their weight of snow
Like a shadow on the shade

Like the beat in your boinger
Like some fisherman boy

Like the fragrance of a lonely season
Like high speed eternity

Like a brown horse now browner
Like marigolds

Like the admiral's ample body
Like a sailor's whiskered ball

2.

Like a half-hearted hobby
Like a pail of herb brew

Like a hand smell
Like a shell smell

Like a tender organ
Like a doggy bag

Like a folded circle
Like an outdoor pee

Like a pressed flower
Like a footprint clue

Like the buttercup trolley
Like ABC moonlight

Sixteen Pickup
Pocket Quarry

Picked up at sixteen

in seventy-five pickup

hand in my pocket

drove me to an Iowan quarry

like an eighties

mellencamp radio

love song then eighteen

on to nineties Kansas City factory

driving around city at night

empty streets smoking

windows down laughing

bench seat boxers

driving one handed

one hand on me

heads and thighs

under streetlight passes

•

2 years and bad streak

of bad luck dropping

out and house fire took everything

christmas party drunk

i set you with my good

friend's ride home

but the ride went to

the wrong house back

to hers & you danced

& she loved your drunken handsome

cowboy body jeans slid them off

crying she said to me next day

all he really did was talk

about you all night

before she got abortion

you'd disappeared

but betrayed wouldn't stick

before your things

were gone i guess

you had too much

else to say in order

to say goodbye

•

Christmas

again, visiting home

three years later driving with sister

in Iowan blizzard

to a farm for a tree

park & you there in snowy

headlight ringing up a pine

my sister asked should we leave

i said no but couldn't get out of car for fifteen

you here xmas tree farm i walk

over to say hi & say hi and

happy surprised to see

me but can't talk at work next night

picked me up at mom & dad's

the drive quiet discussing

places we could go

get a beer & i can't turn my head

from looking out my side

near crying but not

at bar only small talk as friends

not seen for a while but your many quick

drinks said there was more to say

before fight with stranger over

pool & i pulled you out back

to your truck & drove you were drunken to

your mom & dad's got you in

walked home late streets empty the gloomiest

& loneliest i ever felt in my whole life

•

20 years passed

gone & never knowing

then i heard

your brother's head broke

a friend asked if we'd spoken

said now's the time

so wrote:

i'm so sorry

a shortness of breath and

an email back one hour later

asking for phone call i said ok

anytime another email came instead

asking how things are & i tell

my life story realizing the only thing

i'd ever wanted more than

twenty years to share

with you this life who

as a kid thought

could be ours you & me

in the world riding alongside

everything but all of it up broken

in my life I could never

admit equal to everything

I had taken or been given ever since

•

you wrote back said childhood heart

condition caught up late 30s wrecked body

aged fast dr said should not work but odd jobs

pay rent & bills moved to Kansas cattle farm

fell deep with older man also painter

that died & you said afterward could not stop crying

for 5 years now still raising cattle moves very slow

takes many naps just tries to make most

of what you in this one life's given

& said that often still thinks of me has only

wanted my happiness had tried & failed

never wanted it to turn how it did said

now please hope all needs & wants fulfilled

& weighted with deserved pride & said please now push

out what love i'd once put there in these eyes

A Shadow Theater

1.

I'm packing up
my stuff to put
into storage because I needed
to leave my apartment
and live on a commune
with a small group of people
in the woods. When I get there
I see my friend A.,
who is not looking
very healthy, and is not
in a very good mood.
It feels like I have
walked into one of the first
13 colonies. As if I am on Roanoke Island
or something, bad, rotten, sour.
Everyone's nutrition is poor,
supplies are low, people are hungry
and dirty . . . Everyone here
has come for the wrong reasons,
and it isn't working.

I take a lot of walks
by myself. The place is
surrounded by huge fields
with tall grass and trees,
and it often feels like
there are other people out here
with me

that I can't see,
hiding in the brush,
following me. Once when I left
for a walk, someone asked
if I could bring back blueberries
and blue corn chips. They were kidding,
you couldn't find either of those
things for a hundred miles
in any direction.

Part of this commune
butts up to an old cave
with two ends. More like a
naturally formed stone tunnel.
Randomly spaced
along the tunnel's walls
are fist-sized holes that
constantly have a breeze either
blowing in or sucking out
through them. Maybe 8 or 9
holes. At some time
before these new people
arrived, someone had built
beautiful little brass pipe holders,
and drilled them into the cave wall
in front of each of the holes, so that the breeze
blowing through them would always
keep the embers burning in the bowls
of the pipes. When someone walks through
here they will often pick up a couple
different pipes as they pass,
taking a puff from a few
of the different flavored tobaccos.

2.

Me & B.,
and a long blonde hippy couple,
C. and D., whom we've become friends with through
our summer job want to hang out one last time
before summer is over. C. flies hot air balloons
as part of his job here at the camp. We spend the morning
on the beach and in the water.
It feels as though we're the only people on earth.
C. has a couple of hot air balloons with him.
They're broken, but we decide to play
with them anyway. D. isn't great
at working the balloons, but through C.
she knows how to do it a little. But
like, the flame thing is busted
on both of them, and so are the baskets. They were ones C.
had used for work at some point that had gotten broken over time,
and he "thought I'd keep them in the trunk of my car
to play around with in times like this" kind of thing.
We'd all be able to get off the ground a little
in them anyway, and we decide to try and race
each other back home, but we don't get very far. The teams
are me and D. vs. B. and C. Finally, C.
just gets too frustrated that they aren't working well enough
to even play with, and we all stop
and lay the pieces we're each holding
down on the beach. So, now we have to walk
back home instead, and it was a very far walk. Maybe 15 miles.
Sand and dunes and hills all around us. No people, no roads, etc.

We are in the middle of nowhere. D. says to C.,
"you know, at one point . . . a long time ago . . .
there were only like 900 people on Earth. TOTAL."
C. thinks about that for a minute, and shakes his head
with teary eyes, and she says "and everything actually probably
really looked exactly like this," motioning her arms
around her to where we are.

In the loose dry sand, it feels as though
we are walking in place. But, as we walk farther
it starts to get foggy, the landscape begins to change,
and C. begins making these strange visual tricks
in the fog, like shadow puppets in the air.
We were all really impressed
except for B., who seems oddly smug
about the whole thing. Like he knows how the trick works.

We continue through the fog
for the rest of the walk back home,
which continues further with a
forest-like feeling as we get to a paved road
to walk down. I am walking with D, and
the two guys are ahead of us someplace
but we can't see them because of the dense fog.
All of a sudden, maybe 6 feet in front of us
crossing from left to right, is a man dribbling a basketball –
like a phantom basketball player
made out of air. As if the fog had solidified
into a three-dimensional person, running and dribbling
a ball. Then he was back, around behind us,
running and dribbling away. It seems
this is the trick B. knows how to do,

why he's unimpressed with C.'s
shadow puppets from earlier. We all ask how
he does it and he eventually explains
that it has something to do with drawing
in the fog with three-point perspective
rather than just one or two. He then does another
one where he makes these large empty picture frames,
big enough that we can step through them,
that appear to be made out of thick chain,
but really they are made of nothing
but fog. We are incredibly impressed.

While no one is looking I go and try
to tug on the chain, and I'm able to pull on it
and it stretches like a large rubber band, which I figure
somehow reveals the mechanics of the trick
to be false, that it isn't actually just made
out of air and fog. B. catches me doing it,
and he says it doesn't reveal falseness
but instead shows how well
he is able to turn the air
into anything that he wants.
I'm not quite convinced,
it feels a little bit like a rickety
magic trick, like he's talking
through a grin, but they
are completely convinced
by the illusion.

3.

I am part of a group that trades
"New-Age" music cassettes
through the mail, and it happens
that two members of the swap group
are visiting my town at the same time,
so we decide that the three
of us should meet up and make
a swap in person while they're here.
We've never met before, we just
know each other's names from
the long list of people we send
and receive these music cassettes
with, online. None of us
have seen other people in a very
long time, so we're excited
about meeting up.

There are two versions
of our meeting. First, we'll meet
up in a beach parking lot. I drive
my car around the lot looking
for their cars, and I notice that the sand
is creeping really far onto the pavement,
that the edges of the parking lot really
need to be swept back. Then, there is a version
of the meeting where they come over
to my apartment, and I have a joke
I want to tell them while they're

both here, after we've made the swap.

I'll say,
"Well . . . now what should we do?
Do you want to suck my blood?"

I think it's a really funny joke,
but I'm afraid
they aren't going to laugh.

4.

I have a huge pile
of work that I have totally
forgotten about
since the pandemic began.
E. and I had chosen a brand
new series of chapbooks to publish,
focusing specifically on poetry translations.
We had sent out an email
to everyone announcing
the winners and their books,
right before everything shut down.
But the author of the first book
that we are going to do
has gotten sick and I've just been told
that he has died.

I'm trying to figure out
how to contact his family or friends,
but he lived overseas and we
had only ever communicated over email.
Now no one was checking his email.
His book hadn't been finished
when we chose it,
and to release the unfinished work
of a dead man feels . . . problematic.
But to not publish his work
because he has passed away
does also.

There is a book release party
planned for his book at a fancy old theater.
I am there to talk to someone
about cancelling it, and find
two women dressed as fairy ghost
clowns. White faces, long flowing
white dresses and hair, ribbons
tied like headbands around their
foreheads, pink circles
on their cheeks and baby blue
diamonds painted over their eyes.
They are swooping up and down
the long aisles from the stage to the back
of the theater, back and forth,
asking me if this was what I'm looking for.
Apparently they are part of our show,
and are here to rehearse. I tell them
that the author has died, and the show
is going to have to be cancelled.
They look at each other in shock,
moving exactly synchronized,
like mimes looking into a mirror
at their own reflections. I wonder
if this is still their performance.

I just can't understand
how I had forgotten
about all these books,
and I have no idea
how I'll be able catch up,
it feels impossible. I begin to wonder,
if maybe this is all actually a dream?

Did we really set up
this new book series? What about
this big release party? But here I am,
inside the theater, trying to cancel our event.
It all feels very real, not like a dream
at all. But still . . . is this *real*?

5.

I'm on a road trip across the U.S.
and the famous poet F. has invited me
to stay at her house for the night
with her, her husband, and her best friend.
She lives in the country and it's a very hot summer.
F., her friend, and I
are sitting in the living room, talking.
There's a fan on but F.
is sitting right in front of it
with it pointed right at her.
It's not helping the rest of us
very much. A phone in the next room
begins ringing and F. jumps up
to go grab it, right as her friend
asks her a question.
Her friend turns to me and says
that "she's been ignoring me for days now.
I think I might just leave
tomorrow . . . I get the hint."

The house sits on a large sloped field,
a lot of dirt and some crab grass scattered
around. In this field, crows swoop down
and eat newly-hatched penguin chicks,
which I'm told is normal. But what
is particularly upsetting everybody here now
is that they've been eating the older chicks too,
which isn't normal, and they should be stopped.

So, everyone in the house is always casually
keeping an eye on the situation outside,
occasionally yelling at the crows, shooing
them away and throwing small rocks
that are kept in a bowl by the front window.

It doesn't help much. The longer one watches,
the more one realizes that there are hundreds
of penguin chicks, and if a few get eaten
it isn't really the end of the world.
It's more like shooing away the crows
is only something to do on hot days
to pass the time. Sit at the window
and throw rocks at the birds.

Which is what F.'s husband is now doing.
He's sitting on the floor
facing away from me,
hiding underneath a blanket,
looking out the front window.
I get up and walk to the back room
of the house to check it out, and it is much
more like a porch, a type of indoor/outdoor space.
Looking through the windows back there
it looks like night outside.

I turn around and go back
to where her husband is, but
the front wall of the house has disappeared,
and the room is now open
to a different large field
that has a gravel road going across it

about 100 yards away. It's a field
of tall golden weeds. Now F.'s husband
is out sitting on the edge of the road,
in the same position, facing away from me,
underneath his blanket, looking over the tops
of the weeds to the other side of the road.
I can't see what he is looking at,
or hiding from,
so I walk over to him through the field,
slowly, enjoying the dry heat,
the dry golden weeds,
the dryness and crisp texture
underneath my feet as I walk.
The sun feels nice and warm on my skin.
As I approach him, something happens
that I have just missed seeing, but I heard
scuffling on the gravel,
and I look, and *poof!* he's now disappeared.

I look up, and the sky,
which is tan above the golden weeds,
has three or four thin and mysterious
ribbons running through it,
very high up in the atmosphere.
Somehow the turning of the earth,
combined with the intensely heated air,
the planet is reflecting light
in a certain way that makes
these usually invisible
threads in the sky visible
as infinitely thin rainbows.
You can barely even see them,

they are so thin and so very high
up in the sky. As if they were
single threads of spider web,
slowly rocking down
toward the horizon.

Later,
I am a designated
field trip chaperone
for a class of young children,
and we are very lost.
We've been separated from the other groups
of children along a busy road,
and I've gathered the group
onto the grass yard in front
of a new car dealership.
I'm not sure what I should do next.
A little girl from the group
walks over to me and says
that she's going to tell all the other kids
about "the storm," and I say,
"please don't, there's no reason to do that.
You're going to scare everyone."
She turns around to face
the rest of the group and calls
for the kids' attention.
She says, "Everyone see that tree
over there? Now imagine
if that tree *suddenly disappears . . .*"

6.

G. and I are visiting
a mid-sized coastal town
in Spain. It is very touristy, but cute.
The town is having a "gallery night"
where all the galleries coordinated
to have openings on the same evening.
We think we see Meryl Streep
in the passenger seat of a car
at a stop sign. One neighborhood
in town has an option for tourists
to get around by walking on the roofs
of buildings rather than on sidewalks.
So we decide to do that. Roof to roof,
like the way old plague nurses
used to do, visiting their patients.
We get to this very chic butcher shop
that is offering samples of beer,
and we stop to rest our feet and have some.

I can see, piled up on the roof
of this butcher shop a pile of dead human
bodies behind a low cement wall.
The kind of thing one might build
to hide one's garbage cans from view.
I'd guess there might be a dozen bodies.
Their skin had turned completely black
and leathery, like bog people. They are
all wearing straight black cheap Halloween

wigs, the color perfectly matching their skin.
I can see a man's face with no eyes
and a beard. His beard is also a straight black wig,
a bad costume. All of the bodies are dressed
in faded orange linen robes.

I quickly need to sit down
on the bench with my beer,
and I debate with myself about telling
G. about what I've seen.
I do decide to tell her, but I plead
with her not to look. She says she has to look.
I say no she doesn't.
She stands up and walks across the roof
patio, looks back at me, then peeks
over the wall and sees the bodies.
She doesn't say anything, but walks
over to the corner and drops her beer
into the trash can, then calmly walks back
and sits down next to me on the bench.

We get up to pay for our drinks
and get out of here. We rush down the stairs
to the checkout counter, and the butcher
asks us to forgive him for the appearance
of his shop, that it's a bit under construction,
they've just opened. He is in his early 30s,
is very friendly and charming. Asks how we liked
this new beer etc. trying to be a gracious host,
to get people to come to his new business. G. asks
"$5.50, was it? Right?"
We're trying to skip the chatter

and get out of there as fast as we can.
We pay him and rush out.

Walking, we wonder out loud
why there are dead rotten bodies on that roof,
and decide the obvious conclusion is
that he killed them and is butchering them
for his shop. And maybe there is also
the possibility that he is a cult leader.

We also consider that maybe
the roof is being used as storage space
for some local anthropological dig site.
That they need his large coolers, and
have dropped the bodies there for just
a short time while they've gone back
to the site to gather up more corpses.
It's the only other alternative
that we can come up with.

7.

Some neighbors of mine
own an old haunted fishing wharf
that many years ago they built
a restaurant on the end of. They
have hired me to renovate it.
Make the restaurant new and snazzy,
something that might bring in a new
batch of customers during the summer season.
Seems as though my neighbors may
have been behind the haunting all along,
like an old Scooby-Doo episode. It was haunted,
but maybe not as much as they
were making it out to be.
It had been another ploy
to bring in travelers.

So, my main idea for redecorating
their restaurant involves repainting
all of the walls through a single
layer of window screen
that I meticulously staple over every wall,
from floor to ceiling, like wallpaper.
Then I paint the wall, and peel the screen
off once the paint has dried. I feel like
it's a super clever idea, and exactly the type
of thing that will draw in the kind of clientele
they'd like to have. I love the way
it's turning out and I'm really excited
to show the owners, I think they'll love it.

Then the building becomes an antique store
out in the country, with a dusty
old parking lot all around it, very much like
the old Troubadour Books shop
that used to be in Hatfield, MA.
I can now walk around it, rather than
the building being built on the end of a wharf
sticking out into a bay.

I continue to paint the walls.
I'm not quite done with the job yet,
and I grab a blue pea tea bag
out of its box on the shelf in the kitchen,
and wonder how much someone would charge me
for a cup of hot water someplace.

8.

It was late afternoon, and raining,
and just as I'm leaving class (NYU)
I get a text on my phone that says
"Meet me at Julius' Bar?"
But this number isn't saved
on my phone, there is no name
paired with it. I had seen H. earlier
in the afternoon walking down the street
ahead of me, and wonder
if it might be him texting me.
I'm walking through Washington Square Park
and contemplating which direction
I should go, toward the train
or toward the bar. I think,
well, I'm not really friends with H.,
but it seems like maybe he's being friendly
and reaching out . . . maybe I should
go get a drink, say hi.

Inside the bar, the floor
is one long ramp from the door
all the way up to the ceiling,
at the back. It's very dark inside.
I actually do find H. sitting
at a table by himself, but he won't
even look my way. Eventually he does
look up and makes eye contact

with me, then ignores me.
I see no one else here that I know,
so I leave. I have no idea
who texted me.

I leave the bar and go
to a restaurant with a bunch of friends
that are all dressed very goth.
I'm dressed in black
with makeup on my face,
and we're all laughing really hard,
having a lot of fun.
The waitress is a friend
of ours, and she keeps bringing
us free refills on our sodas
and lots of french fries.
We're sitting on a long couch
with a table in front of us,
like a long one-sided booth.
The owner of the restaurant
comes over to our table and says
"I have a great idea for my favorite
customers, let's move this seat
to our very special VIP section for you!"
So, the cooks and waiters and all these guys
show up from out of nowhere, all dressed
in white chef's clothes, like 50 of them,
and they pick up this super long couch
and just turn it around so it faces the wall.
There's no way to sit on it
anymore, but they are all quite proud

of this idea they had for us. We stand
around looking at each other
holding our fries and drinks
wondering what we should do.

9.

I'm travelling alone,
and go to visit Martha's Vineyard
for a little while. I'm by far
the youngest person there.
In a fussy little trinket shop
full of knickknacks and antiques,
I introduce myself to the owner,
a lady named Martha Vineyard,
just like the island.
We become fast friends.

Eventually, I meet some
of her other elderly friends
there at the shop too, and one
day when there's a little group
of us there chatting and gossiping
around the counter, Martha says
"oh my gosh, look what I have..."
and she pulls a ceramic platter
off of a shelf in the store
that has 4 sheep painted on it.
Above the sheep their names
have been hand-painted. The first sheep
is Don, then Molly, then Ben, then Martha,
lined up in a row.
I realize all 4 of us here
have recognized our own names
on the platter. It is a crazy coincidence.

I then turn and say to the old man,
"Oh wow, my dad's
name is Don."
He says to me, "funny,
my son's name is Ben!"

Later, Martha commissions a painting
from me, and she asks for me
to use the colors rust, dark green,
and chocolate brown. The painting
has something to do
with her own death. A gift to herself.
"It's her last painting," her friends say.

When I try to leave
the shop I can't find
my shoes anywhere.
Whenever anyone comes
into the shop they are asked
to remove their shoes, and mine
aren't by the door
where I had left them.
I try to put on another pair
to wear as I walk around
the store looking for my own,
but the owner of the shoes
I'm borrowing catches me
putting his on, and he follows me
around, wondering what I'm doing,
worried that I'll steal his.

I find an enormous room,
it's a "lost and found" of shoes.
Tons of them, lined up,
in maybe 20 rows, like a cemetery,
I think. The whole floor of the room.
I eventually do find a pair of my own
there, but they are not
the shoes that I had worn in.
They're my rubber snow boots,
and they're covered in dried mud,
but definitely mine.
So without asking any questions
I quickly put them on, and leave.

10.

I am one person in a group
of maybe 15 people who are going
into an unmapped wilderness.
Lush fields, canyons, forests, etc.,
all of it at a natural scale, but all of it
completely constructed, not natural. Built.
We are undercover and searching
for trees that have been planted
as grave markers, looking to find
the bodies of an earlier group
of our explorers that had come
before us, to recover their bodies
and bring them back home. The trees
they had planted to mark their own graves
had already grown tall. It had been many years,
so these trees were all mixed in
with the forests that had been built,
so we have to search
through them very carefully,
looking for *our* trees.

During this recovery
mission the story flips, and now
we are looking for our own spots
to plant the tree seeds that we have brought
with us, to mark our own gravesites.
We have all gotten very sick. There is a woman
who went off on her own and we can't find her,

but we can hear her. She is saying:
Come get me! Come get me!
But her voice is soft and muffled and
it is foggy, and we can't find her anywhere.
Then, like a movie, there is a shot of us
walking in a single-file line over foggy hills,
with her voice overdubbed saying:

I came here knowing what to do.
I needed to go underground.
I needed to go deep inside a hole
that led deeper into a smaller hole,
that led even deeper into the ground,
and into a smaller hole
that led to an even smaller hole,
until the opening is just big enough
for me to crawl inside of it and fit
my body into the pouch.
Once inside it,
deep, deep, underground,
I'm one of the thousands.
There will be no difference
between my body and the pouch.
There will no longer be
a hollow cavity inside the earth,
my body will fill it perfectly.
It was made just for me.

11.

I'm part of a theater company
out in industrial Brooklyn, and
the owner of it, J., who is a super old friend
of mine, asks if I'd help him burn it down.
No one was going to see plays
there anymore, and they are losing
all their money. But mostly, it's because
J.'s just not interested
in doing it anymore.
So I said ok, and I help him
set it on fire.

But he also lives there,
so he's homeless now, too.
Standing on the sidewalk
I see the huge tower of smoke
coming out and I'm like *whoa*
we really did it, what is he going to do.

Then of course we have to come up
with a fake story to tell
the rest of the theater company –
but the thing is that the fire
got him a lot of media attention,
he was on the tv news and online,
and all these people started donating
a bunch of money to a gofundme to help
him rebuild a brand new theater –

even though he didn't want one anymore.
But he couldn't say that
he had started the fire himself. So,
because more people now knew
about the theater, because of all the publicity
and everything, people started looking
into the work they had done in the past,
and it actually became this kind of famous place,
and the brand new theater
was really fancy and people loved going
to it, and they all started winning awards,
and it turned out J.
really loves being famous.

12.

I've been invited to visit
a Middle Eastern country
by a man I know named K.
He's invited me over
in order to show me around
"before everything changes."

He picks me up at the airport,
and as we're driving into town
he's talking about these giant paintings
of suns that I will see
put up all around the capital city,
high up in the sky
above the buildings
by Donald Trump.
He thinks that politically it is very smart,
but "we do actually have seasons here,
and that doesn't really seem
to have been taken into consideration
by the U.S. government."

He's driving me around over dunes
and through old buildings,
there aren't really any roads, and I wonder
how that might change the way I'd think about things.
You just go in straight lines
from place to place. Apparently K.

has some sort of political power
here, because he's taking me into rooms
where government meetings are taking place,
showing me fancy jewelry
under cases etc. Because I'm with him
though, security doesn't check me.

At one point we are driving along the water
and I see L. standing with a group
of people out in the ocean,
she's also flying a kite. I knock
on the car window to get her attention
even though she's far away from the car,
but she actually does hear me
and waves, but then yells at me
to not bang on the glass so hard
because I might break it.
She yells "how stupid, Ben!"

K. drives me to a beautiful palace,
we're quietly sneaking around
the hallways and there are a lot
of servants we need to hide from.
He sneaks me into a room
that is a pristine white cube, like an art gallery,
with one long shelf going round the whole room.
There are little clay and wooden sculptures,
maybe 100 of them, spaced around on the shelf.
K. says "I knew it! The queen
has been stealing the children's artwork.
See, if she would just ask,

the kids would be honored
to have their art here
in the palace. They would all be
so proud."

13.

Watching old tv show
bloopers on YouTube, I
come across a video
of a recently-found "lost"
Seinfeld blooper. I click
to watch it, and it's a scene
being shot on a big
wooden deck behind a beach
house. The house is on the left,
then there's the large deck
in the middle, and there are steps
on the right that go down
to the beach. It is all
on a big sound stage. A party
scene was just being shot,
and the director and crew are telling
the extras and the actors
to go on out to the beach while they set
everything up again for the next take.
The deck needs to be cleared off.
There are a lot of extras, it is a big
party scene, and slowly everyone
begins walking toward the steps
to go out on the beach, they are all
chatting and laughing and taking their time,
but the camera keeps rolling.

I start picking out faces
in the crowd: there is an old woman,
there is a group of ladies
in bikinis, I see "Elaine" talking
to a crew member looking
at papers as they walk,
I see "George" talking
to some guy as they slowly
walk toward the beach,
and then, in between
the people of the crowd, I see
a figure standing in the very
far back of the set that isn't walking,
he's just standing
looking at the camera.
I can only catch glimpses
of this person in between
all of the other people, but somehow
I have a way of playing the YouTube
video in slow motion, and I can also
zoom in – and when I do I get
a clear view of a man hiding
in the background of this crowded
scene, wearing a black suit,
with a mechanical silver robot face,
wearing a perfectly combed
brown wig. He can see me
watching him through the video
and I get very very scared.

14.

There are two houses on either side
of a large field. I walk across it,
from one friend's house to another
friend's house. Some wooden steps
go up the side of a hill, up to the front porch
of the second house. This house is at the very top
of the hill, hidden behind trees. Once on the porch,
I can see M. through the screen door,
and she pushes the door open for me
and gives me a hug and invites me in.
I say "long time no see," and she smiles
and says she's been eating a peach tart
in the kitchen, and that I
should eat some too before it's gone.
There are people here that I know, visiting
from out of town, and we say hi. Friends of friends,
I don't know them well. The light in the house
is mid-evening dim, no light on but not quite dark.
Someone is playing guitar and singing
quietly in one of the bedrooms down the hall,
where their door is open. I think there are three or four bedrooms,
and visitors are staying in each of them.
It's not an empty house. One level, old, and it's used
for people visiting, for friends of friends. A guest house.
I go into the kitchen and a small woman with very short,
very blonde hair is rubbing some Vick's Vaseline
on her wrists and I say *ooh I love that stuff* and she says "me too."
I rub some on my arm and sniff. M. asks what it is,

what it's used for, and this lady tells her. M. shrugs
and takes a big dip of it, puts it on a hairbrush
and runs it through her hair.

Everyone is about to leave to go to the house
I had walked over from, on the other side of the field.
I'm here to pick everyone up, to let them know
we're ready for them to come over now. I try to put my shoes
back on by shoving my feet into them, but they're still tied
and I can't get them back on. I need to sit down
on the couch and do it right, so I do, then go down
the steps and out into the field.
Streetlights are starting to turn on.

Because of the time it took me to put on my shoes
correctly, I'm walking by myself, behind everyone else
as we cross the field to the other house – which has now
changed into an indoor/outdoor bar that is open
on one side like a car repair garage. The side facing us is open,
I can see inside. I can see that my friends are
the only people there so far, and they're standing around
the pool table playing "strip pool," like strip poker, but shooting pool.
Many of them are already almost naked. I walk in and see N.,
he's not playing pool, but instead sitting with a drink
at the bar. I sit next to him and say hi. He says "you're so coy . . ."
with a big grin on his face. I say "coy?" He nods.
He says "you love a good fight." I ask "I do?"
He nods and says "like that day on the beach. . . . ?"
I say I remember (but I don't, actually) and say
"well that's a totally different story. . . ."

Later, I am driving a car and then riding my bike
through hilly East Davenport neighborhoods.
Sometimes it's icy. I have to take the garbage out,
down a long path from a house to the road for someone
that lives there, but is out of town. I am housesitting for them.
Then I am walking around the three big stone mansions
in that same neighborhood, up above the Mississippi River.
I dreamt my family at one point lived in one,
it was the house that I had grown up in maybe, and it was
intensely haunted and very scary. It had always been *saturated*
with ghosts, and there were some parts of the house that we didn't
even use because of it, where the dead people lived.
SO MANY dead people. We just pretended that those parts
of the house weren't there. Like, on the 2nd floor, the entire left side
of the house was locked up. We wouldn't go in there, but originally
it had been my space. We had to lock it up. But really, the whole house
was haunted. I could remember specific rooms of the house
while I walked around in the yard outside, and I was feeling
pretty scared. Now, the house is empty, and people are looking
at buying the house next door.

Two houses separated by a big yard.
I was both out walking around
in the yard with the possible buyers,
telling them about our old haunted house
next door, and inside of it, watching us
from out of its front windows.

15.

The weather is beautiful today,
sunny but not hot, and
a lot of people are outdoors
to enjoy the day.
I'm in a city, maybe it's Tokyo,
and everyone speaks English
but they are from countries all over the world.
I have a job selling fabric
at a fabric store and as a drug dealer
outside of an ice cream parlor
in my neighborhood. Everyone has to have
at least two jobs these days.
I sell a little white pill,
like, half a tic-tac, and it
makes people laugh for about 20 minutes.
I have friends that work
at the ice cream parlor, it's why
I hang out there. We all
have really crazy cartoon cars
that we drive around town, with every
window a different color of glass,
with hologram tinting and lights.
Mostly we just sit on the bench
outside the ice cream parlor and watch
the fancy dogs that the people of Tokyo
own. Really elaborate haircuts etc., and
I am a virtual encyclopedia of dog breeds.
I can tell anyone anything

about any kind of dog. At one point
one of my friend's dogs is walking
with us, and it's the size of a caterpillar
on a leash, and I'm scared
I'm going to step on it because
it keeps walking so close to my feet.

Later, I am a teacher
at a boy's boarding school,
and I'm hanging out in the large
dorm room of four of my students,
in their late teens. They live
in the attic of one of the old buildings.
The school is way out in the country,
in Scotland maybe, rolling green hills
all around us. Pete Buttigieg
went to school here, and the boys
are talking about him saying
he's on campus today to give a lecture.

Then the world ends.
It is now me and Pete
and an older woman who works
as a secretary in the school's
main office, and we are trekking
through a barren landscape.
We come upon a village of mud
and adobe huts but there are no people left.
Eventually, we get to a huge cliff
where we can see really far, and it looks
like *Lord of the Rings* with all the scary mountains
and valleys and lightning and lava

down below us. Pete and the woman
both agree that we have to keep going higher.
I say "Higher? There is no higher,
we're on the edge of a cliff, we have
to figure out how to go *down*,
and make our way through
that scary valley." They both agree
that it's way too dangerous to try do that.
"We have to keep climbing up."
But I say, "Aren't we going to have
to go down at some point though?
Why go higher now? This really feels
like we're going in the wrong direction . . ."
I know going through the valley
will be fine, it just looks worse
from where we're
standing.

16.

Some of O.'s coworkers and I
go to a restaurant at night,
after they have closed. An older
woman dressed like an old
schoolmarm meets us, and she's
the owner. She leads us
to a back room
behind the dining room,
usually reserved for private events,
and there is a model city
built on a large table.
Like a huge sprawling train set
without a train. I'm pretty sure
it is a scale model of New York City.

I am both
looking at the city from above,
and I am small and inside
the model city itself, which
now feels life-sized. The older lady,
the restaurant owner,
grabs a handful of steel ball bearings,
and she tosses them into the model,
maybe it's a pinball machine? The ball bearings
fly down the streets
and bounce off of the buildings
making an enormous racket.

It's the middle of the night
and I am walking in a college town,
I think Amherst, MA, and there is
no one on the street but me and a teenage girl.
I am walking about 20 yards behind her,
but she keeps making the same turns
that I'm going to have to make, so
it's beginning to seem to her
like I'm following her. But I'm not –
we're just going the same direction.
I can tell she's starting to feel scared
and she starts walking faster
and I stop walking and pretend
to look into the windows of a closed store,
to let her go on ahead for a while. The sound
of her clicking shoe-steps get quieter
as she gets further away, and soon
there are no sounds at all, nothing,
and the little town suddenly feels fake,
like a movie-set or something.

17.

I'm in a South Asian country
and it's hot and humid. I've hired a boy
to be my cricket trainer, for my professional
sporting cricket. At sunset I rush back
to the stadium stepping over scorpions
on the sidewalk to tell the boy & cricket
to spend the night there because
it's still very hot out, and there are a lot of scorpions
on the sidewalks. Scorpions love to eat crickets.
On my walk back to my hotel
I stop and watch a puppet show
depicting stories of the history of the country
I'm visiting. It is a huge production in a large oval
theater with people sitting all around.
It's like a circus, how there are many stories going on
at the same time. They are telling the stories
of military battles, it's very sad and dramatic
and everyone is crying, me too. The final story
is about the town where we all currently are,
where 100 years ago they had a messenger come
tell them that this beloved farmer 5 miles away
was being harassed by thugs, so all the men rushed off
on their horses to go defend him – but it was a trick,
and they had left their town defenseless and the thugs
came in and killed all the women and children
and burnt it to the ground. Everyone in the audience
was very upset. Somehow the stadium
where the cricket games were happening

played a part in the story too. It is a historical landmark,
the only building in town that hadn't burnt down.

When I get back to the hotel
my parents are there too. I have my own bed,
but we are sharing one room. The lights are off
but they are lying awake talking. Just then something
my dad says sets off the Alexa, which thinks
he has asked it something about S&M, so it starts
giving all these resources for S&M techniques
very loudly in the hotel room, in the middle of the night,
turned all the way up because my dad has terrible hearing
and has to have the volume on the highest level.
My parents are laughing really hard. After they get it
turned off my mom says that a female friend
of mine had called to say that they were at a local bar, but
she didn't get her name. She asks if I was going to go meet them
and I say no, I am too tired. I lay down to go to sleep,
and watch the shadow of a tree
in the green rectangle of light
on the wall.

Acknowledgments

Some of the poems in *12 Folded Poems* were first published in the chapbook *Three Folded Poems*, (The Song Cave, 2019).

Thanks to Jason Evans, some of the dreams in *A Shadow Theater* appeared, in a different form, on his website *This Long Century* (www.thislongcentury.com).

OTHER TITLES FROM THE SONG CAVE:

1. *A Dark Dreambox of Another Kind* by **Alfred Starr Hamilton**
2. *My Enemies* by **Jane Gregory**
3. *Rude Woods* by **Nate Klug**
4. *Georges Braque and Others* by **Trevor Winkfield**
5. *The Living Method* by **Sara Nicholson**
6. *Splash State* by **Todd Colby**
7. *Essay Stanzas* by **Thomas Meyer**
8. *Illustrated Games of Patience* by **Ben Estes**
9. *Dark Green* by **Emily Hunt**
10. *Honest James* by **Christian Schlegel**
11. *M* by **Hannah Brooks-Motl**
12. *What the Lyric Is* by **Sara Nicholson**
13. *The Hermit* by **Lucy Ives**
14. *The Orchid Stories* by **Kenward Elmslie**
15. *Do Not Be a Gentleman When You Say Goodnight* by **Mitch Sisskind**
16. *HAIRDO* by **Rachel B. Glaser**
17. *Motor Maids across the Continent* by **Ron Padgett**
18. *Songs for Schizoid Siblings* by **Lionel Ziprin**
19. *Professionals of Hope: The Selected Writings of* **Subcomandante Marcos**
20. *Fort Not* by **Emily Skillings**
21. *Riddles, Etc.* by **Geoffrey Hilsabeck**

22. *CHARAS: The Improbable Dome Builders* by **Syeus Mottel** (Co-published with Pioneer Works)
23. *YEAH NO* by **Jane Gregory**
24. *Nioque of the Early-Spring* by **Francis Ponge**
25. *Smudgy and Lossy* by **John Myers**
26. *The Desert* by **Brandon Shimoda**
27. *Scardanelli* by **Friederike Mayröcker**
28. *The Alley of Fireflies and Other Stories* by **Raymond Roussel**
29. *CHANGES: Notes on Choreography* by **Merce Cunningham** (Co-published with the Merce Cunningham Trust)
30. *My Mother Laughs* by **Chantal Akerman**
31. *Earth* by **Hannah Brooks-Motl**
32. *Everything and Other Poems* by **Charles North**
33. *Paper Bells* by **Phan Nhiên Hạo**
34. *Photographs: Together & Alone* by **Karlheinz Weinberger**
35. *A Better Place Is Hard to Find* by **Aaron Fagan**
36. *Rough Song* by **Blanca Varela**
37. *In the Same Light: Poems For Our Century From the Migrants & Exiles of the Tang Dynasty*, translations by **Wong May**
38. *On the Mesa: An Anthology of Bolinas Writing (50th Anniversary Edition)*, edited by **Ben Estes and Joel Weishaus**
39. *Listen My Friend, This Is the Dream I Dreamed Last Night* by **Cody-Rose Clevidence**
40. *Poetries* by **Georges Schehadé**
41. *Wings in Time* by **Callie Garnett**
42. *Two Murals* by **Jesús Castillo**
43. *Punks: New & Selected Poems* by **John Keene**